JAMES JOYCE

THE *FINNEGANS WAKE* NOTEBOOKS AT BUFFALO

A Reader's Guide to the Edition

BREPOLS PUBLISHERS

Publication of this volume was assisted by The Baird Foundation, Buffalo, New York;
The Office of the Provost, University at Buffalo, The State University of New York;
Institut des Textes et Manuscrits Modernes (CNRS); The University of Antwerp.

D/2001/0095/88

ISBN 2-503-50956-2© Images by the Estate of James Joyce, 1978

Editing Joyce's Notebooks

Overview

The *Finnegans Wake* notebooks are the last major body of work by James Joyce to remain largely unedited. Of the nearly fifty surviving authorial notebooks only two—VI.A and VI.B.46—have been published in full, the latter over two decades ago. Apart from these, all of the published transcriptions have been piecemeal ones, yet our understanding of the nature of the notebooks has developed greatly in the intervening period. What made most of the more recent transcriptions possible was the publication of the *James Joyce Archive* in 1978. The significance of this event for Joyce studies can hardly be overstated. Black and white facsimiles of virtually all of Joyce's manuscripts were now available to scholars in major libraries throughout the world. The impact was at first gradual but cumulative: genetic and manuscript studies began to play a much more dominant role in many of the Joyce journals, such as the *Newslitter* and even the much more theory-based *James Joyce Quarterly*. This period also saw the personal computer revolution of the eighties, and the arrival of the Internet and email in the nineties: computers allowed much more efficient organisation and analysis of manuscript transcriptions, while the new forms of instant communication created cohesion among the widely scattered groups of researchers. All of these developments have made it possible for us to undertake the massive task of publishing a complete critical edition of all the extant workbooks compiled by Joyce after the completion of *Ulysses*.

Joyce's writing in the notebooks is often so difficult to decipher that a facsimile without a transcription is of limited use for most readers. Simple transcriptions would also be inadequate since many notebook entries have no independent meaning apart from their origin and eventual destination (this was a problem faced by many readers of Thomas Connolly's *Scribbledehobble*). The vast majority of them are notes taken by Joyce from a remarkable variety of written sources, for indeterminate use at first and then for insertion in particular sections of his 'Work in Progress'. The notebooks also contain many personal notes and observations (not all of them for compositional use), but the distinction between personal observation and source-derived note is not always self-evident and in many cases can only be properly understood after all possible sources have been investigated.

To make sense of the notebooks, one must therefore try to understand the dual logic of Joyce's compilation and use of his materials. It is essential not only to identify as many sources as possible, but also to trace the usage of the entries in the drafts.

The potential source material read by Joyce is of extreme diversity, mixing the profound and the trivial in equal measure. Some of it is so obscure and ephemeral that it is almost miraculous that so much has survived. Were it not for the farsighted policies of institutions such as the British Library—which set about collecting and preserving schoolgirls' novelettes with the same zeal that was accorded to what were judged to be canonical works—many of Joyce's sources would probably never have come to light. Nevertheless it is also likely that some sources will remain tantalisingly elusive, although we hope that the present edition will encourage readers to discover many new ones. We have tried, however, to provide, for each notebook, a sufficiently substantial proportion of source identifications and a representative account of draft usage. The sources are quoted extensively, so that readers will be able to assess for themselves how or why Joyce would have selected particular words and phrases, and enough of the draft context is given to allow readers to draw their own conclusions about the rationale of the insertions.

Descriptions and analyses of the notebook entries are supplemented by a reduced black and white image of each notebook page, placed in close juxtaposition with its transcription, while larger colour images of the most interesting openings are reproduced in an appendix. It is hoped that this will enable readers to check and challenge the editors' readings.

Draft transcriptions

Ideally, the present transcriptions will eventually link up with a complete critical edition of the drafts: in the meantime, our purpose is not to anticipate such an edition, but simply to give an idea of the usage of the notebook material. We quote the form of the item as it is inserted in the draft and the immediate draft context, where it is sometimes distinct from the notebook form and often very different from the final form it will assume in *Finnegans Wake* (if indeed it reaches that stage). The mode of insertion of the item and its position on the page are indicated by a code: it is genetically important to know if a word has been integrated directly into the main text of a draft, substituted in a fair copy or added to a typescript. Should readers wish to examine the draft for themselves, the code should also help them to locate the item on the often very crowded page.

Within the limits of a project focussed on the notebooks, only a few lines could be devoted to the draft situation of each item, so transcriptions have been simplified and no attempt has been made to render the full complexity of the documents. Whereas the notebook transcriptions have been checked several times against the originals in Buffalo, it has not always been possible to check the draft readings against the manuscripts in the British Library.

Notebook Titles and Sequences

Later work by Roland McHugh and particularly by Danis Rose and John O'Hanlon has established a much more precise time frame and dramatically reshuffled the sequences determined by Peter Spielberg (the opening run of titles is now VI.B.10, VI.B.3, VI.B.25, VI.B.2, VI.B.11), but the Spielberg titles have by now been firmly established and we have decided to retain them for our transcriptions.

Our publication sequence is dictated by a number of practical considerations, such as the amount of work that has already been accumulated on individual notebooks. We have also tried to give priority to the early notebooks: these are of particular interest, as they show Joyce in the process of discovering the themes, characters and organisational principles that will make up not only the building blocks, but the ground-plan of the *Wake*.

Transcribing Joyce's Notes

Joyce's notes, it has often been pointed out, were written not for publication but for his own use. In contrast to the neat hand of his fair copies we find here for the most part writing that is merely a means of getting words on to paper as quickly as possible, often under adverse circumstances. On the evidence of a number of mistranscriptions it would seem likely that at least some of the time Joyce had others read his sources out to him, while he hastily jotted down whatever struck him as useful or interesting. Words are often scribbled in a way that amounts to a sort of shorthand: standard endings, such as 'ing' or 'ed' are frequently reduced to a flourish. On some occasions, while recovering from eye operations for example, Joyce turned to a page already containing notes and wrote further notes over these. Add to all of this Joyce's frequent scorings of transferred units in dark blue crayon and the result is a formidable challenge. Yet, bearing these considerations in mind, it is perhaps surprising to find that only a small percentage of the notes has resisted decipherment.

Faced with prima facie illegible entries, our chief guides are Joyce's predominantly objective and rational procedures regarding compilation and use of his material. If we are able to place a note within a sequence taken from a source, or locate it in a draft, the meaning frequently shines forth at once. In all such cases our approach is to take the intention for the deed, to render whole words as we deduce them and to avoid cluttering the transcriptions with indications of intermittent illegibility. These last we reserve for entries which we cannot match satisfactorily against a source or draft and whose readings leave some residual doubt.

Definition of Units

Joyce's notebook entries are divided editorially into *units*: a unit may be defined as a word, a line, part of a line, or several consecutive lines that are construed to constitute a distinct and discrete item of meaning.

The editorial treatment of these depends on a number of factors. Discernment of some units may appear to be self-evident. For example, a single word, or self-contained phrase on a single line, such as the first line of VI.B.10.034, 'Introduction 700pp', can usually be assumed to be a unit. Often Joyce will divide units by means of a short interlinear horizontal stroke. Further indications may be provided by the position of a unit or part of a unit on a page, or by a change of writing implement. For example, where a unit occupies two lines, the second line is very often indented, as in 'toucan bird smaller than / own beak', also on VI.B.10.034. But in the majority of cases the source of the note and its subsequent use will be determinative. Again on VI.B.10.034 we find the words 'Shee Crinion / Colthurst' on two consecutive lines, the second of which is indented. Joyce has marked the conclusion of the preceding group of notes with a horizontal stroke running across the 'C' of 'Crinion', but no further strokes occur until several units later. 'Colthurst' has been cancelled in red, but it is quite common for part only of a unit to be crossed.

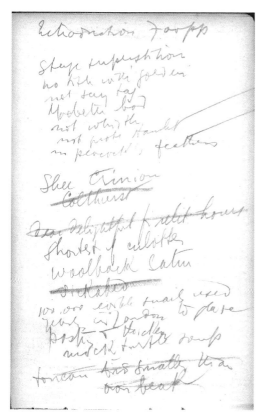

VI.B.10.034

A clear thread running through the early notebooks is Joyce's interest in personal names, and the unit(s) would seem most likely to belong to this category. One might also speculate on the significance of 'Colthurst', the name of the insane British army officer who murdered Joyce's friend Francis Sheehy Skeffington. Without further information there appear to be two possibilities: 'Shee Crinion / Colthurst' or 'Shee Crinion', followed by 'Colthurst'. Location of the source—the *Irish Times* for 17 November, 1922—demonstrates that there are in fact *three* separate units: 'Shee', 'Crinion' and 'Colthurst', the first two of which happen to be on the same line.

Often there will be more than one layout option. There are many instances of clusters of items from a common source which have either not been used at all, or which have entered contiguously into the same draft and which survive in reasonable proximity in the published text of *Finnegans Wake*. In those cases, we aim at the simplest representation. To take an example: although they appear on the same line, the first three words on VI.B.10.089, 'flint, chert, obsidian', are clearly distinct objects and items of meaning. Had they gone into more than one draft location, or had they been derived from widely separated passages in the source text, it might have been necessary to put them on three separate lines. In the absence of these conditions they can be conveniently treated as a single unit.

Annotation

We have appended notes to those aspects of the transcriptions that seem to call for comment. Most of the notes provide short glosses on Joyce's entries. It is notoriously difficult to establish satisfactory principles in this area. What one reader may find useful another may regard as insultingly obvious. Joyce's readers are as likely to be found in Tokyo and Beijing as in Dublin, Paris and New York. Accordingly, we have translated foreign words familiar to many English speakers and identified placenames and historical figures that Europeans may take for granted.

When confronted with obscure notebook entries for which no source has been located, we have tried to confine our glosses to whatever factual information we can glean, leaving speculation to our readers. In such cases, finding a source which reveals the true derivation of a notebook entry can prove a chastening experience. For example, VI.B.10.56 has the entry 'de Sales La Terriere', just a few lines below a reference to St Luke. St Francis de Sales died in 1622 and some newspapers for 1922 contained articles on his tercentenery. It was easy to assume that Joyce had taken his note from one of these, and that the unexplained item, 'La Terriere', had something to do with the life of St Francis. In fact, as we later discovered, the note had simply been transcribed from the Births column of the *Irish Times* for 27 November 1922:

> De Sales La Terriere. Nov 21 1922 at Kiltinan Castle, Co. Tipperary, the wife of F.J.B. De Sales La Terriere, M.F.H., of a son.

In some cases we have added a speculative gloss, prefaced by an interrogation mark. More often, when the significance of a note is unclear, we have omitted comment altogether.

Cross-references

We have not attempted to cross-reference all appearances of the larger themes of *Finnegans Wake*, or the more prominent members of its cast of characters, although readers should find much of this information in the selective indexes to each individual volume. We have sought to indicate the reappearance in other notebooks of more specific items, such as the repeated use of a source text, or related lists of words or names, but such notes are contingent on our present incomplete knowledge of the whole body of the notebooks.

For a number of notebook entries we have given selective references to Joyce's other works, but readers may disagree about what is genuinely useful here. For example, the note at VI.B.10.031*e* reads: '1753 Barry Yelverton / (lord Avonmore) in / Trinity'. This has been taken from the *Irish Times* for 8 November 1922, where an article on the 'College Historical Society in Trinity College' tells us that 'In 1753, Barry Yelverton, afterwards Lord Avonmore, started a debating society, called the College Historical Club, but of its proceedings no record remains.' Here we include a reference to the appearance of Mrs Yelverton Barry at *Ulysses* 15.1013, which may help account for why this particular item caught Joyce's attention. On the other hand, *Ulysses* has an encyclopedic sweep, alluding to almost every aspect of Irish history and much else besides, so it was felt that many cross-references would take up much additional space without necessarily leaving readers any better informed.

Joyce's Colour Crayons

The editors of the *James Joyce Archive* attempted, under impossibly restrictive conditions, to give a summary account of Joyce's use of colours in crossing through notebook items. This led to some simple errors (green for blue or red, for example) which are quite straightforward to correct. Yet, even after repeated examination of the original manuscripts, Joyce's use of various shades of red and orange remain extremely difficult to distinguish, which in turn raises the question of whether Joyce himself was always able to distinguish them. As the colours represented successive forays into the notes for use in the drafts, we checked them against the various draft levels and found that the different shades were often used as part of the same transfer session. This led to the conclusion that Joyce would have had a number of crayons set aside for each colour. As one became blunt he could quickly reach for a sharper one without having to break his concentration. There is also evidence that he occasionally got his colours mixed up, so that he might unintentionally pick up a blue pencil while cancelling items in green, or vice versa. See, for example, the group of notes in VI.B.3, 024*f*, 027*e*, 040*i*, 072*b*, 073*a*. These were almost all cancelled in blue, for use in *transition* 12, with the exception of 040*i*, where green was used. On the other hand, notes transferred from the same notebook to *transition* 13 (061*d*, 063*a*, 068*a-b*, 109*b*, 136*f*) were green-cancelled, with one exception (061*d*) cancelled in blue. Our procedure is to represent the colours as simply as possible, according to use, and to ignore nuances of shading unless they can be shown to have a clear relation to specific drafts.

History of Notebook Research

The study of Joyce's *Finnegans Wake* notebooks started in the early fifties, when Peter Spielberg began to catalogue them after their acquisition by Buffalo University. In his study of the relationship between Joyce and Mallarmé, David Hayman used notebooks as well as manuscripts. In 1961 Thomas B. Connolly published the first full notebook transcription in *James Joyce's Scribbledehobble: The Ur-Workbook for 'Finnegans Wake'*. In the same decade the newly established *A Wake Newslitter* began to publish short studies on the notebooks, and microfilm copies were circulating at least from 1964. Leo Knuth published a series of in-depth studies of language lists in the notebooks and in the April issue of 1971 Roland McHugh presented the first identification of a source in a notebook. Both language lists and sources remained the focus of attention of notebook scholars. These interests were combined one year later in the first monograph: in *Joyce et Rabelais: Aspects de la création verbale dans Finnegans Wake,* Claude Jacquet included a transcription of notes that Joyce took in VI.B.45 of L. Sainéan's *La Langue de Rabelais*. The notebooks were also central to Roland McHugh's study of the *Finnegans Wake* sigla in 1976.

Two years later David Hayman and Danis Rose published facsimiles of all the notebooks in Michael Groden's *James Joyce Archive* and Rose also published a complete edition of VI.B.46. This period saw *A Wake Newslitter* increasingly taken over by notebook studies and when the *Newslitter* ceased to exist this became the main focus of *A 'Finnegans Wake' Circular*, edited by Vincent Deane. In the meantime too, the French genetic scholars became increasingly interested in the *Wake* notebooks. In the nineties the notebooks became a central object for study of a number of different groups: David Hayman returned to the topic with a number of articles and a book and both the Parisian ITEM and Geert Lernout's group in Antwerp organised conferences, produced dissertations, published articles and edited collections of essays, including a number of special issues of *European Joyce Studies*. In addition individual scholars like Joe Schork and Jorn Barger and electronic collectives such as the different *Finnegans Wake* lists, among them Mikio Fuse's, have contributed greatly to our understanding of the nature of the notebooks and thus to this editon. Luca Crispi and Sam Slote, 'Joyce Scholars in Residence' at Buffalo and Françoise Antiquario, Ingénieur d'études at CNRS, have assisted in all stages of the preparation of the present edition.

Website

The editors are keenly aware that an ambitious project such as an edition of the *Finnegans Wake* notebooks can only be effective if it is cooperative from the very beginning. The finding of sources for Joyce's notebook entries is one of the tasks for which we would like to ask our readers' help. The Antwerp James Joyce Centre has set up a website where we will post specific queries about notebook entries. We will offer a transcription of the relevant page(s) and a list of the books and articles that have already been discounted as possible sources. All help is welcome and, needless to say, will be acknowledged in both the printed and the electronic edition, as well as on the website itself.

ADDRESS: http://ger-www.uia.ac.be/webger/ger/GJS/QUERIES.htm

In addition the electronic journal *Genetic Joyce Studies*, also on the Antwerp centre's website, will publish articles, background materials, a 'Work in Progress' timeline, a bibliography of genetic criticism and other tools that may be of help to present and future collaborators.

Vincent Deane, Daniel Ferrer, Geert Lernout

Bibliographies

Joyce's Works
(based on the *James Joyce Quarterly* List)

CP	Joyce, James. *Collected Poems.* New York: Viking Press, 1957.
CW	Joyce, James. *The Critical Writings of James Joyce,* ed. Ellsworth Mason and Richard Ellmann. New York: Viking Press, 1959.
D	Joyce, James. *Dubliners,* ed. Robert Scholes in consultation with Richard Ellmann. New York: Viking Press, 1967.
	Joyce, James. *'Dubliners': Text, Criticism, and Notes,* ed. Robert Scholes and A. Walton Litz. New York: Viking Press, 1969.
E	Joyce, James. *Exiles.* New York: Penguin, 1973.
FW	Joyce, James. *Finnegans Wake.* New York: Viking Press, 1939; London: Faber and Faber, 1939. These two editions have identical pagination.
GJ	Joyce, James. *Giacomo Joyce,* ed. Richard Ellmann. New York: Viking Press, 1968.
JJI	Ellmann, Richard. *James Joyce.* New York: Oxford Univ. Press, 1959.
JJII	Ellmann, Richard. *James Joyce.* New York: Oxford Univ. Press, 1982.
JJA	*James Joyce Archive.* Eds. Michael Groden, Hans Walter Gabler, David Hayman, A. Walton Litz and Danis Rose. New York: Garland, 1978. See last two pages of *JJQ* for guide.
Letters I, II, III	Joyce, James. *Letters of James Joyce.* Vol. I, ed. Stuart Gilbert. New York: Viking Press, 1957; reissued with corrections 1966. Vols. II and III, ed. Richard Ellmann. New York: Viking Press, 1966.
P	Joyce, James. *A Portrait of the Artist as a Young Man.* The definitive text corrected from Dublin Holograph by Chester G. Anderson and edited by Richard Ellmann. New York: Viking Press, 1964.
	Joyce, James. *'A Portrait of the Artist as a Young Man': Text, Criticism, and Notes,* ed. Chester G. Anderson. New York: Viking Press, 1968.
SH	Joyce, James. *Stephen Hero,* ed. John J. Slocum and Herbert Cahoon. New York: New Directions, 1944, 1963.
SL	Joyce, James. *Selected Letters of James Joyce,* ed. Richard Ellmann. New York: Viking Press, 1975.
U	+ episode and line number. Joyce, James. *Ulysses,* ed. Hans Walter Gabler, et al. New York and London: Garland publishing, 1984, 1986. In paperback by Garland, Random House, Bodley Head, and Penguin.
	+ page number. Joyce, James. *Ulysses,* ed. Hans Walter Gabler, et al. New York and London: Garland, 1984. References to Foreword, Critical Apparatus, Textual Notes, Historical Collation, or Afterword.

General Reference Works

Banta	Melissa Banta and Oscar A. Silverman, eds. *James Joyce's Letters to Sylvia Beach: 1921-1940.* Bloomington: Indiana University Press, 1987.
CE	*The Catholic Encyclopedia.* 1913.
Dinneen	Rev. Patrick S. Dinneen, ed. *Foclóir Gaedhilge Agus Béarla: An Irish-English Dictionary, New Edition, Revised and Greatly Enlarged.* Dublin: The Irish Texts Society, 1927.
DNB	*Dictionary of National Biography*
11th EB	*The Encyclopædia Britannica.* 11th ed. 1910.
EDD	Joseph Wright, ed. *The English Dialect Dictionary.* Oxford: Henry Frowde, 1905.
OED	*The Oxford English Dictionary*, ed. James Murray *et al.*, 2nd ed. Oxford: Clarendon Press, 1989.
Grove	Stanley Sadie, ed. *The New Grove Dictionary of Music and Musicians.* London: Macmillan Publishers Limited, 1980.
Joyce, P.W.	Patrick Weston Joyce. *English As We Speak It In Ireland*, reprint, with an introduction by Terence Dolan, of the 1910 edition. Dublin: Wolfhound Press, 1979.
Moylan	Séamus Moylan. *The Language of Kilkenny: Lexicon, Semantics, Structures.* Dublin: Geography Publications, 1996.
Ó Muirithe	Diarmaid Ó Muirithe, ed. *A Dictionary of Anglo-Irish: Words and Phrases from Gaelic.* Dublin: Four Courts Press, 1996.
Partridge	Eric Partridge. *Dictionary of Slang and Unconventional English,* edited by Paul Beale. 8th edition. New York: Macmillan, 1984.
Traynor	Michael Traynor. *The English Dialect of North Donegal: A Glossary.* Dublin: The Royal Irish Academy, 1953.

Key to Transcriptions

General

The notebooks are named according to the system devised by Peter Spielberg in *James Joyce's Manuscripts and Letters at the University of Buffalo*. Each title begins with a roman numeral: the VI series comprises the notebooks relating to *Finnegans Wake*. These divide further into four categories:

VI.A: A single large, atypical notebook, mainly in Joyce's hand, later known as *Scribbledehobble*, after its opening word, and published by Thomas Connolly under that title.

VI.B.1-40, **42-48**: The primary series, which consists of forty-seven small notebooks in various formats, written in Joyce's hand. VI.B.48 was compiled after *Finnegans Wake* had been completed.

VI.B.41: Notes written by Joyce at the end of VI.C.18 (see below).

VI.C.1-18: Eighteen notebooks containing transcriptions by Madame Raphaël of unused material from the B series and used in the same manner as the B series.

VI.D.1-7: Virtual notebooks. These represent parts of VI.C.1-18, whose originals in the B series are no longer extant.

Pagination

Most notebooks do not have their own pagination. This edition generally follows the numbering introduced by the *James Joyce Archive* (abbreviated *JJA*), but translated into 3-digit format: 001, 002 etc. The following abbreviations are also used:

fcr	front cover recto
fcv	front cover verso
ffr	front flyleaf recto
ffv	front flyleaf verso
bfr	back flyleaf recto
bfv	back flyleaf verso
bcr	back cover recto
bcv	back cover verso

Some pages, unnumbered in the original notebooks, have become detached, and were numbered conjecturally in the *James Joyce Archive* (*JJA*). In certain cases it has been possible, with the aid of evidence such as source texts or earlier records and on the basis of a revised bibliographical description, to establish a more likely page order. In such cases the *JJA* page number is replaced with the new number, but this latter is immediately followed by the *JJA* number in square brackets. For example, the opening page of B.10 is labelled as follows: 'VI.B.10.001 [002 in *JJA*]'.

Notebook Entries

Notebook entries are printed in bold type. To facilitate reference we have tagged the units alphabetically as follows: (a), (b), etc.

Symbols

/	A virgule is used to indicate line breaks when material on successive lines forms part of the same unit. Virgules are used similarly in transcriptions of sources, to indicate text on successive lines, and in some sources, such as newspapers, to divide a transcribed headline from the main text. In the draft transcriptions, they indicate a change of paragraph.
//	A double-slash indicates a page-break, when material on successive pages forms part of the same unit.
~	A tilde at the end of a line indicates that the next unit follows without a line break. This is a common feature of certain notebooks, such as VI.A and VI.B.46.
>	Where several otherwise discrete units derive from the same passage in the source text, they are divided by a chevron (>) and the source passage is cited only after the final unit of the group. Chevrons are also used to divide successive notebook units that share a common gloss, the gloss being placed immediately after the last unit of the group.
>>	A double-chevron marks a page break within a group of units deriving from the same source or sharing a common gloss.
(>) (>>)	In cases where the grouping of units is conjectural, the chevrons are placed within parentheses.
}{	Used in combination with virgules to represent tabular layout, where the notebook entry has a number of words on consecutive lines placed in juxtaposition to a single word, or further group of words, on a single line or on consecutive lines. See below for a more detailed discussion with examples.
~~Cancellation~~	Deletions are indicated by strikethrough.
[ ]	These enclose editorial comments. When placed around the FW location of a unit they indicate that the unit has been obscured by subsequent revisions and is only partly represented in the finished text.
[…]	Editorial ellipses are enclosed in square brackets. Ellipses that are in the sources or in notebook entries are reproduced without brackets.
^+…+^	Caret-plus and plus-caret are used to mark respectively the beginning and end of inserted material. They may also be nested to indicate insertions within insertions.
[ ]	Italicised square brackets enclose an editorially construed transcription.
?	Prefixed to a MS location or gloss, this indicates that it is speculative.
[?]	Illegible part of word.
[??]	Illegible word.
+	Joyce occasionally returns to an already inscribed page and adds further units. These later insertions are marked with a superscript +.

Joyce occasionally clusters notes in quasi-tabular form, placing one word or phrase (which often functions as a defining label) in juxtaposition with a number of words on successive lines. For example, on VI.B.10.062 'dormy', 'stymie', 'niblick' appear on successive lines, and on the right of this list 'golf' in brackets spans all three lines. This is transcribed by having the line endings represented by the usual virgules and by a brace pointing from the group to the individual unit juxtaposed with the group. Our example from VI.B.10.062 appears as follows:

dormy / stymie / niblick } (golf)

The same principle is extended for several groups, or several individual words in juxtaposition with one or more groups. For example, on VI.B.10.064 two phrases, 'can't say' and 'don't know', are juxtaposed with '(I)' on the left and '(Cycl)' on the right. This is represented as

(I) {can't say / don't know } (Cycl)

With groups of units, Joyce sometimes uses dashes to represent ditto signs, as in the following example:

'farmers' shoots / rough — ing'.

Double vertical strokes, resembling the more common ditto marks, have been standardised and all instances represented by dashes.

Sums and calculations in the notes are rendered analytically as single line equations wherever possible.

Although Joyce often separates units by short horizontal strokes, his practice is not consistent. Since readers can inspect these markings on the reproduced pages, they have not been transcribed.

Superscripts

Joyce uses a series of coloured crayons and slate pencils to cross through notebook entries for transfer to his drafts. Each note crossed through in this way has a superscript bold-italic letter prefixed to it, indicating the colour of cancellation.

> *b* = *blue*-deleted material; *bk* = *black*-deleted material; *br* = *brown*-deleted material; *g* = *green*-deleted material; *o* = *orange*-deleted material; *p* = *purple*-deleted material; *r* = *red*-deleted material; *y* = *yellow*-deleted material.

Cancellation

In some notebooks, such as VI.B.29, cross-throughs do not indicate transfer, but have the status of corrections, or clarification of units that are difficult to read. The crossing-through in these cases is usually in the same pen or pencil as the note itself and followed by a replacement unit.

When crossing-through takes place within the same level as the notation (currente calamo), the deletion is indicated by strikethrough thus: ~~old unit~~ new unit.

Where the crossing-through appears to be part of a subsequent revision process (usually indicated by interlinear additions, different writing utensils or a clearly later hand) the substitutions are surrounded by carets and plus-signs thus: ~~old unit~~ ^+new unit+^.

Where Joyce has crossed through for draft use an item already cancelled as part of a revision process, this is represented with a combination of superscript and strikethrough, thus: *o*~~cancelled unit~~.

Joyce's Sources

Most of Joyce's notes are taken from written sources, such as books, or articles in periodicals or newspapers. The title and page references of each source text are placed directly below the notebook entries derived from them, followed by citation of the passage used by Joyce.

Source citations are preceded by the source name and then, where called for, volume, page, column reference in that order. Cross-references to the use of the same source in other notebooks are given in the bibliography.

Citations are not placed between quotation marks, but when the source text itself contains an opening quotation mark this is reproduced. Where the quoted matter has been abbreviated a closing mark is supplied, preceded by an ellipsis.

Wherever possible the source citation will have the exact features (spelling, punctuation, etc.) of the original. There are, however, some exceptions. Formatting of such features as newspaper headlines, and the use of bold type have been normalised. Caps in headlines are replaced by the normal style for titles. The only punctuation retained at the end of a citation is a period, where this also occurs in the passage cited. Where a citation has been abbreviated, leaving a sentence incomplete, all other closing punctuation (comma, semi-colon, etc.) is omitted.

An ellipsis in the source is reproduced as is. Editorial ellipses (like any other editorial interventions) are enclosed within square brackets.

For the *Oxford English Dictionary* (abbreviated as *OED*), in the few cases where it is cited as a source, the headword is followed by the sense number. For example, VI.B.30.082(a), 'Finner / (whale)' is glossed as follows:

> *OED*, 'Finner' 1: A name given to whales of the genus Balænoptera, esp. the Rorqual, from the fact of their having a dorsal fin.

For citations from the *Catholic Encyclopedia* (*CE*) and the *Encyclopædia Britannica* (*EB*), the article title is followed by the page number together with the alphabetic code used by the editors of those works to qualify the page references. According to this system 'a' represents the top half of the first column; 'b', 'c' and 'd' respectively refer to the bottom half of the first, and the top and bottom halves of the second column. For example, a reference to the *Encyclopædia Britannica* article on 'Stockholm', would be cited as 11th *EB*, 'Stockholm' 935a if the unit was taken from the upper left quadrant of the page.

For newspapers or periodicals, the title and date of issue are immediately followed by the page/column reference; the citation is preceded by the title of the article in square brackets. The following example cites a passage from the *Irish Times* for 21 October 1922, which is to be found on column 6 of page 5:

> *(b)*   **franking machine**
>
> *Irish Times* 21 Oct 1922-5/6: [Stamps of the Future] The "Philatelic Magazine" received yesterday, was in a wrapper franked by a three-halfpenny stamp impressed in red by an automatic postal franking machine.

Draft Information

When a notebook unit has been transferred by Joyce to a draft of his work in progress, the place and manner of insertion are described as shown in the following example:

> *(e)*   ʳrest assured >
>
> MS 47482b-15v, LPA: I'll break his face for him ^+rest assured,+^ | *JJA* 57:032 | probably Apr 1924 | III§1A.*/1D.*1//2A.*1/2C.*1 | *FW* 442.16

As can be seen, this contains a series of items separated by vertical bars.

1. Manuscript reference followed by draft quotation

The MS folio and page references (usually British Library) are given as follows:

> MS [folio]–[page] (for example: MS 47483-100).

The Manuscript reference is immediately followed by a short citation, showing the notebook unit as it first appears in the draft. To help the reader locate the unit on the draft page, an approximation of its position is indicated by a series of abbreviations:

BMA   Bottom margin addition

BMS   Bottom margin substitution

EM   Extradraft material

ILA	Interlinear addition (includes addition between paragraphs)
ILS	Interlinear substitution (includes substitution between paragraphs)
LMA	Left margin addition
LMS	Left margin substitution
LPA	Left page addition
LPS	Left page substitution
MT	Main text
OS	Overwritten substitution
RMA	Right margin addition
RMS	Right margin substitution
TMA	Top margin addition
TMS	Top margin substitution

The following abbreviations are also used to qualify the preceding codes:

Ins	Insert
Pr	Printed page (proofs, galleys or transition).
	Example: PrTMS: top margin substitution on proofs.
Scr	Scribal.
	Example: ScrLMS. scribal left margin substitution
Ts	Typescript.
	Example: TsILA: interlinear addition to typescript.

Transcription of Draft Insertions

The purpose of these transcriptions is not to give a complete representation of the manuscripts but to provide a simplified representation of the context and manner of insertion of the notebook items.

Additions are enclosed as follows between combined carets and plus signs: ^+additions+^. The asymmetrical form allows a less ambiguous representation of nested insertions.

Deletions are indicated by strikethrough (even if the deletion on the manuscript is not done by means of crossing out): ~~deleted element~~.

Substitutions are indicated by a deletion immediately followed by an addition (overwriting is also represented in this way): ~~old element~~ ^+new element+^.

Whenever possible without misrepresentation, a holistic picture of the operation will be given. As a rule, single letter modifications will be represented as whole word modifications: '~~ear~~ ^+bar+^' rather than 'e^+b+^ar'.

The drafts of *Finnegans Wake* include a number of episodes that were abandoned or recycled. These are 'Tristan and Isolde', 'The Revered Letter', 'The Delivery of the Letter', and 'Scribbledehobble'. Where Joyce has used recycled draft material, either from worksheets or discarded drafts, this process is represented, following the model above for the constituent parts. In these instances the data for both insertions are given, linked by the symbol [→], in the following format:

> MS 47481-94, LMA: in her oceanblue brocade with iris petal sleeves ^+and an overdress of net darned with gold+^ | *JJA* 56:002 | Jul 1923 | II.4§1.*0 | 'Tristan and Isolde' [→] MS 47481-113v, LPA: 16. tootyfay charmaunt in her ensemble of maidenna blue, overdress of net, tickled with goldies, | *JJA* 56:170 | late Aug 1938 | II.4§2.8/3.8 | FW 384.31

2. *James Joyce Archive*

The *James Joyce Archive* contains facsimiles of almost all the extant manuscripts of *Finnegans Wake*. For each manuscript listed, the *JJA* volume and page references are given.

3. Date of usage

This indicates, as accurately as possible, the date when the notebook unit entered the draft.

4. Draft code

Finnegans Wake is divided into four books, which are in turn divided into chapters: the first has eight chapters, the second and third have four, the fourth consists of a single one. However, the text was not originally conceived with this plan in mind. It began as a series of episodes, which eventually went to make up sections, which were in turn combined to make up the finished chapters.

The draft code begins with a roman numeral from I to IV, identifying one of the four parts. For books I and II this is joined by a period to an arabic numeral identifying the chapter within the book (for example, I.1, I.2, I.3; II.1, II.2, II.3 etc.). The book-chapter codes are followed by the sectional symbol § and followed in turn by a series of numeric-alphabetical codes indicating chapter sections, joined by a period to a number indicating the (chronological) draft level. Where a draft stage of a chapter comprises a number of linked sections, these are joined by virgules. For example: 'I.6§1.9/2.6/3.12/4.8' can be read as indicating a particular draft level of *Finnegans Wake*, part I, chapter six, which subdivides into four sections, joined by virgules: section 1, draft level 9, section 2, level 6, section 3, level 12 and section 4, level 8. The relevant section is underlined. For instance 'I.6§1.9/2.6/3.12/4.8' indicates that the notebook unit entered the draft in section 2 (FW 139.15-28).

As the fourth book consists of a single chapter, the roman numeral IV is immediately followed by the sectional symbol §. For example: IV§1.3/2.6, which indicates a draft of book IV that is made up of the third level of section 1 and the sixth level of section 2.

The representation of the third book is slightly complicated by the fact that here the *Archive* treats the chapters themselves as sections, so the roman numeral III is immediately followed by the sectional symbol §, further subdivisions being indicated by combining the chapter number with a letter of the alphabet. For example: III§1A.5/1D.5//2A.5/2B.2/2C.5. Here the chapter divisions of the finished text are indicated by double virgules. This, then, represents a stage at which the text consists of the fifth level of sections A and D of chapter 1, along with the fifth level of section A, the second level of section B and the fifth level of section C of chapter 2.

The reader is referred to Danis Rose's introductions to Volumes 44 to 63 of the *James Joyce Archive* for a full discussion of draft coding conventions.

5. *Finnegans Wake* page and line reference

For *Finnegans Wake* page-line references the text used is the 1964 Faber edition of *Finnegans Wake* (this differs by a line from the Viking edition on pages 548-54). References are rendered in the five-digit form used by Clive Hart's *Concordance*. For example, line one of page three is '*FW* 003.01'.

Where a unit has undergone a radical transformation, so that it may only be discerned in part in the published text of *Finnegans Wake*, the reference is placed in square brackets.

Where a unit from a recycled draft, or extradraft sheet, has failed to make it into the text of *Finnegans Wake*, this is indicated by the sign '[*FW* 000.00]', the process being represented as follows:

MS 47481-95, ILA: a favourite lyrical bloom ^+bellclear+^ in iambic decasyllabic hexameter | *JJA* 56:008 | Aug 1923 | II.4§1.*1 | 'Tristan and Isolde' [*FW* 000.00]

Missing drafts are marked as 'MS missing' under MS, and all available information about them is given. Unlocated units are indicated by the formula: 'Not located in MS/*FW*'.

6. *A First Draft Version* page and line reference

Where the unit has not survived into the finished text, but may be found in David Hayman's *A First Draft Version of 'Finnegans Wake'*, the *FDV* page and line reference is given. Where the draft readings in our transcription differ from the *FDV* readings, this is recorded in a note.

Marginal Units

Marginal units are ordered in the most rational sequence determinable. For example a source may make it clear that Joyce took the notes in a certain order but ran out of space. In such cases the sequence of the source is followed. Otherwise the transcriptions of marginal units are placed after those of the units on the main body of the page. Any special features, such as their status as later additions, are indicated by a superscript + or discussed briefly in a note.

Notebook to notebook transfers

In a small number of instances, units from the VI.B notebooks have been transferred from one notebook to another. For these the page number is given. For transfers to VI.A, the section heading is also given, as in the following example:

> *(k)*   *bk***Old Top,**
> *Leader* 4 Nov 1922-306/2: [As Others See Us] Cheerio now, old Top.
> VI.A.0721 ('Oxen of the Sun')
> MS 47480-267, ILA: after the last King of all Ireland ^+the old top that went ^+before him+^+^ | *JJA* 55:446a | Jul 1923 | II.3§7.*0 | *FW* 380.21

Where an entry (normally unused) has been transcribed by Mme Raphael into one of the C notebooks, a reference is given. The notebook number is cited, followed by page number and unit tag, in standard form as follows: 'VI.C.09.020(a)'.

Uncancelled units not transcribed by Mme Raphael into the C series are labelled as 'Not transferred' and a reason may be offered in an appended note.

In some cases an uncancelled unit entered the draft history, and was also transferred by Mme Raphael. Here the C reference is given as before, immediately under the *JJA* draft code.

For three of the notebooks—VI.B.8, VI.B.17 and VI.B.20—the unused units have been transcribed into two C notebooks. Here the addresses of both C notebooks are given, in chronological order, separated by a semicolon.

Editorial note

Buffalo notebook title and page number

Notebook unit

Source text excerpt

Chevron indicating continuation of source text between consecutive notebook units

VI.B.10.006

Notebook unit, alphabetically tagged

(a)   **to wind hounds >**

      Note: Wind. To perceive (an animal, a person, or thing) by the scent conveyed by the wind.

      VI.C.5.096(b)

Source of unit with abbreviated bibliographical data and page reference

(b)   **⌐runs down wind**

      Quarterly Review Oct 1922, 273: [Reynard the Fox] When hunted, [the fox] cares little about being able to see or hear his pursuers as long as he can wind them.[…] It is for this reason, of course, that he habitually runs down wind

      MS 47482b-63, MT: the bulbul down the wind | *JJA* 58:005 | probably Nov-Dec 1924 | III§3A.*1 | *FW* 476.02

(c)   **coombe >**

      VI.C.5.096(c)

(d)   **batch >**

      Notes: Batch. The vale of a stream or rivulet.

      Joyce's note is followed by a pencil stroke resembling a circumflex accent and probably equivalent to the interlinear lines.

      VI.C.5.096(d)

(e)   **mosshykes >**

      Notes: Moss-hag. Broken ground from which peat has been taken; a pit or hole from which peat has been dug.

      The 'k' of Joyce's entry crossed by symbol resembling that described at (d) above.

(f)   **drumming of snipe >**

      Note: Drum. Of birds or insects: To make a loud hollow reverberating sound, as by the quivering of the wings.

      VI.C.5.096(f)

(g)   **morass >**

      VI.C.5.096(g)

(h)   **⌐pointing for his kennel**

      Quarterly Review Oct 1922, 273-4: [Reynard the Fox] One May morning about sunrise […] I was watching for badgers in a West Dorsetshire coombe […] Flanking the steep sides of the 'batch' to right and left of me, stretched extensive gorse-breaks […] while dividing the breaks from the larch coverts ran a ribbon of silver-grey marsh land, flecked with […] bright emerald excrescences […] suspiciously like moss-hags.[…] For some time I watched the peculiar gyrations of a snipe, which since the first streak of dawn had been rising and falling in its own peculiar way, drumming incessantly all the while.[…] Along a faint sheep-path, which skirted the morass came a beautiful dog-fox […] Full fed, and therefore at peace with all things, he was pointing for his own kennel, somewhere in one of the breaks.

      Note: Point. Of a hound: To indicate the presence and position of (game) by standing rigidly looking towards it.

      MS 47471b-28, MT: he last was viewed pointing for home | *JJA* 46:047 | probably Nov-Dec 1923 | I.4§2.*0 | *FW* 097.12

Notebook unit, alphabetically tagged

Source of unit with abbreviated bibliographical data and page reference

Transferred unit: C series notebook address

Superscript indicating colour of cross-out of notebook unit

Cameo image of notebook page

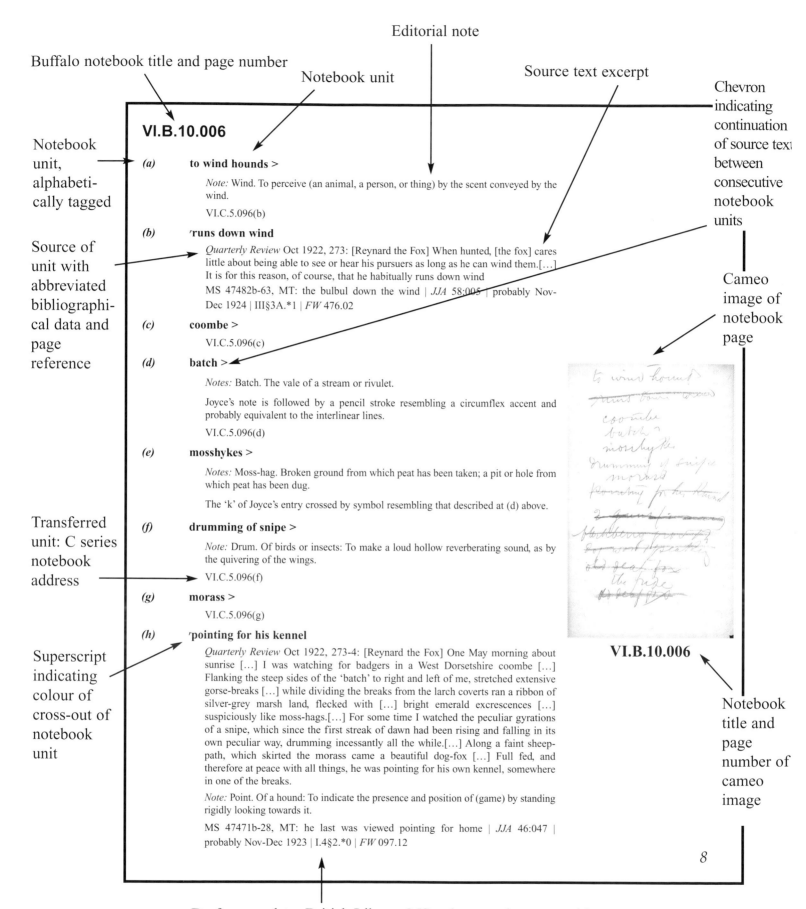

VI.B.10.006

Notebook title and page number of cameo image

8

Draft usage data: British Library MS volume and page; position on page; draft reading; *James Joyce Archive* volume and page; date of draft insertion; draft level; *Finnegans Wake* citation

16